A Catholic Wedding Plan

Project Management Style

By

Pádraig Boyle

Boyle Practical Project Management

© 2020 BPPM

www.bppm.ie

1 A Catholic Wedding Plan

This book provides the detail needed to plan a traditional Catholic wedding within a period of at least 8 months. This plan attempts to cover all the detail associated with planning a Catholic wedding to assist the Bride and Groom. It does not promote any supplier and the project plan author has only the interests of the Bride and Groom in mind. This book serves as a roadmap and as with all weddings the Bride and Groom will ultimately decide on a route that suits them best.

1.1 Initiate Wedding

The Bride and Groom plan to get married within the next two years and have a church wedding followed by a reception. A wedding is a project that has a fixed date and therefore fixing the wedding date is the 1st order of business.

1.1.1 Fix Date

The process used for fixing a wedding date is dependent on the Bride and Groom priorities. The fixing of the date is generally dependent on the availability of their chosen church, reception venue and band. The earlier the planning commences the better the chance of satisfying all the main priorities.

1.1.1.1 Book Church & Priest

The Bride and Groom decide on a day of the week that they would like to be married. Saturday weddings are popular mainly because it tends to suit most guests and for this reason, they tend to be more difficult to arrange and can be more expensive. They meet with the parish priest or their preferred celebrant at least 8 months prior to the dates they have in mind to establish his and the church availability. They note all the suitable dates the church and the priest are available and will be told what requirements that religious body has, to get married under their rites.

While a religious marriage ceremony can be performed according to the custom and rites of the religious body, there are certain requirements dealt with later that must be met for the marriage to be legal

1.1.1.2 Book Reception Venue

The options for the number of suitable venues are reduced based on personal preferences of the Bride and Groom. Some couple may prefer a castle while others may prioritise a venue with a view to minimizing the amount of travel guests have to undertake. Couples have held their receptions in a marquee in the ground of their homes'. The ambiance and the atmosphere surrounding such a setting can add to the occasion. There is a considerable amount of extra planning required for the marquee option. For example, organising caterers, permits, electricity power supply, parking, and toilet facilities. Catering companies normally can supply waiting staff, bar service, catering equipment, furniture, crockery, linen etc.

The Bride and Groom research potential reception venues to determine average prices and services on offer. They visit a selected number of venues based on location, services on offer, price, and advice from friends. They establish the potential reception venues available dates. The Bride and Groom would normally have an approximate number of guests as this may impact on the choice of venue. The table below is a sample of criteria

A Catholic Wedding Plan - Project Management Style

used for illustrative purposes that may assist in selecting a venue.

Criteria	Unit Measure	Reception Venue		
		1	2	3
Distance from the church	k/metres	15	30	40
Bride/Groom experience	Mark 1-10	9	8	10
Family & friends experience	Mark 1-10	8	8	9
Price main meal	Per head	50	45	60
Price wine reception	Per head	8	12	10
Price evening food	Per head	10	12	13
Guest capacity.	Min./Max.	50/600	50/550	50/500
Special overnight guest rates	Discount	0	10	15
Limitations for music	Finish Time	02.00	01.00	02.00
Bar closing time	Finish Time	01.30	02.00	01.30
Performance space band	Sq. Metres.	25	30	40
Sound limiters	Yes/No	No	No	Yes
Baby changing facilities.	Yes/No	Yes	Yes	Yes
Band changing facilities	Yes/No	Yes	Yes	Yes
Secure place for gifts	Yes/No	Yes	Yes	Yes
Areas for photographs	Yes/No	Yes	Yes	Yes
Guests parking	Yes/No	Yes	No	Yes
Wheelchair access	Yes/No	Yes	Yes	Yes
Table centrepiece	Yes/No	Yes	Yes	Yes
Red Carpet	Yes/No	Yes	Yes	Yes
Cake Stand	Yes/No	Yes	Yes	Yes
Extra charges	Yes/No	No	No	No
Wine corkage charge	Per bottle	0	1	2
Deposit % of total	Amount	10%	10%	20%
Cancellation policy	Loss	Deposit	Deposit	Deposit

3

Figures entered are for demonstration only. The Bride and Groom take everything into consideration before they decide on a reception venue.

1.1.1.3 Musicians Availability

The Bride and Groom may prefer a particular band or maybe a band that can perform a mixture of material to cater for all age groups that would include traditional, rock, pop, country, and soul music. They may require the band to accompany singers from among the guests and entice people on to the dance floor. In general, couples want a band with the experience to perform the appropriate material at the appropriate time at the right price.

When there is no one preferential band, the Bride and Groom start searching based on initial preferences, and recommendations from family and friends. They note email addresses and phone numbers of potential bands for further enquiries.

Preparing a list of questions as outlined below to ask bands in advance, helps narrow down the number of bands fitting requirements. They email or phone each band for answers to the questions and gather any other relevant information. The table of criteria below is a sample for illustrative purposes that may assist with selecting a band.

Criteria	Unit Measure	Band		
		1	2	3
No. of Playing Hours	No. Hrs	2	2.5	2
Sample live DVD	Yes/No	Yes	Yes	No
Travel Charge	Yes/No	No	No	No
Other Charges	Yes/No	No	No	No
Total Price	Money	2,000	2,200	2,700
Deposit	%	10%	10%	20%
Leeway on Start Finish	Minutes	30	45	30
No. of Breaks	Number	1	2	1
Length of Break	Minutes	20	15	15
Details of Referees	Yes/No	Yes	Yes	Yes
Weddings Performed	Number	5	30	10
List of Available Dates	Yes/No	Yes	Yes	Yes
Sound Limiters Issues	Yes/No	Yes	Yes	No
Space Requirements	Sq. Metres	30	30	30
Food Requirements	Type	Buffet	Buffet	Buffet
Drinks Requirements	Yes/No	No	No	No
Changing Facility	Yes/No	Yes	Yes	No
Set up Time	Minutes	30	45	30

The Bride and Groom attend a few public venues to listen to the music of potential bands. They ask the bands about availability, price and if they were performing at any upcoming parties or weddings. It is good practice to see a band perform at a wedding or a party to verify their credentials and experience before making the booking. Be aware that the members in a band may be interchangeable and the band you choose may be the band you get but the band members may be different.

1.1.1.4 Family Availability

Prior to making any final decision on a date the Bride and Groom notify their respective immediate families and close friends of the available dates to ascertain if there might be any known events occurring that may compromise any family member or close friend.

1.1.1.5 Project Charter

This Charter gives authority to commence project planning for Bride and Groom's wedding.

Goal

The over-riding Goal of the wedding is to get married and the purpose of the wedding is to

    a. Form Voluntary Union
    b. Receive Sacrament
    c. Celebrate the Occasion

Stakeholders

The primary stakeholders are Bride and Groom, their Family, Friends, Wedding Guests, and the Priest.

The secondary project stakeholders are the Parish Administrator, Wedding Venue Staff, Band, Photographer, Videographer, DJ, Driver, and Florist.

The Budget

The budget for the wedding is set by the bride and groom exclusive of the honeymoon.

Timescale

The product completion date is the date of the wedding. The project completion date can be a couple of months after this date.

1.1.2 Success Framework

The Bride and Groom determine that the basis for a successful wedding is through satisfying success criteria. The critical success factors are represented in the middle of the theoretical success framework diagram, representing their relationship to achieving both project and product objectives and their influence on satisfying the success criteria. The objectives, the success factors and the success criteria are agreed between the Bride and Groom and the parish priest.

1.1.2.1 Project Outputs

The project outputs or objectives are:

Comply with Regulations	Fulfill Religious Requirements
Deliver within Timeframe	Operate within Budget

1.1.2.2 Critical Success Factors

The Critical Success Factors are:

- Clear Objectives

Set out the outputs or objectives in a clear and understandable fashion such that all activities undertaken can be targeted at meeting those objectives. The scope of the wedding is more easily kept on track and controlled with clearly defined objectives.

- Operational Services Selection

Take due care with selecting and procuring the required services and contractors.

- Project Management

Put all the ingredients in place and apply all the knowledge, tools and techniques to the wedding as outlined in this document to meet requirements.

1.1.2.3 Success Criteria

The criteria as set out in the table below measure the success of the project based on the project outputs.

Project Outputs	Details	Time in Months from Wedding Day	Measure Unit.
Comply with Regulations	Complete Legalities	6 before	Marriage License
Fulfill Religious Requirements	Complete Catholic Pre-Nuptial. Enquiry	2 before	Church Service
Deliver within Timeframe	Activities Completed	1 after	%
Operate within Budget	The Cost of All Activities	1 after	Cost

1.1.2.4 Risks

The risks, their likely impact and the necessary response are outlined in the table below:

	Risks	Impact	Response
1	Wet Weather	Adverse effect on Wedding Party Dress & Photos	Prepare for wedding party wet weather comfort and location for wet weather photos.
2	Bridal Party Transport Fails to Show.	Major Delay with Ceremony	Send Reminder text day before. Schedule Transport to arrive at bride's home at a certain time. See contingency for use of family cars.
3	Priest Delayed	Delay with Ceremony	Reminder text day before. Schedule Priest to arrive at church 20 minutes prior to wedding time.
4	Priest Fails to Show	No Ceremony	Prepare for alternative celebrant.
5	Musicians Delayed	Delay with Start of Music	Arrange for musicians to check in with groomsman at least 45 minutes prior to the anticipated start time.

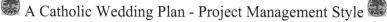

	Risks	Impact	Response
6	Musicians Fails to Show	No Music	Make plans for alternative musical entertainment.
7	Photographer or Videographer Delayed or Fails to Show	Quality of Photographs	Make plans for alternative photographer or videographer from the guest list.
8	Troubles with Wedding Party Clothes or Footwear	Quality of Appearance	Identify qualified resources in advance to rectify and have emergency kits
9	Vendors go out of business	Loss of deposit. Extra cost of alternatives	Review wedding insurance options and credit card terms.
10	No Wedding Rings	Panic	Purchase alternative cosmetic jewellery rings and give to family member to bring to church

Risk No. 1. Wet Weather

Have a supply of large umbrellas, all the same size and design available for use by the wedding party. One of the groom's party can arrange to have these stored at the houses from which the Bride and Groom are leaving from. The brollies can be put into the vehicles transporting the bride and groom for use later if required. If not required for the weather the brollies can be used as props for photographs if so desired. The contingency is for the photos to be taken at a pre-selected weatherproof venue. Include "areas for photographs" as a selection criterion for the reception venue.

11

Risk No. 2. Bridal Party Transport Delay

Put a process in place to get the bride to the church in the event of Bridal Party Transport not arriving. For example, a relative, neighbour or friend with appropriate transport can be requested to remain at the bride's home until the bride leaves and may like to follow the bridal car to the church. The selected relief transport driver transports the wedding party to the church, from the church, to the photograph's location and the reception if required.

Risk No. 3. Priest Delayed

The priest is expected at the church 20 minutes before the wedding. In the event of him not arriving and if there is no other priest con celebrating the wedding put a process in place to determine the cause and duration of delay. For example, in this event [Groomsman Name] rings the priest and notifies [Bridesmaid Name] of expected delay. For this to happen the groomsman needs to have the phone number for the priest and the diocesan administrator.

Risk No. 4. Priest Fails to Show

In the event of the priest not showing up at all and if there is no other priest con celebrating the wedding put a process in place to find a replacement. For example, in this event [Groomsman Name] contacts the diocesan administrator [Phone number] to arrange an alternative celebrant. [Groomsman Name] will notify [Bridesmaid Name] of expected delay.

Risk No. 5. Musicians Delayed

In the event of the musicians not arriving at a given time [Groomsman Name] is to ring the band at [number].

Risk No. 6. Musicians Fails to Show

The Bride and Groom compile contact details for alternative local bands and musicians that could potentially perform at short notice. [Groomsman Name] is to contact local bands from the precompiled list.

Risk No. 7 Photographer or Videographer Delayed or Fails to Show

In the event of the Photographer /Videographer not arriving at the bride's house at a given time [Bridesmaid Name] is to ring the Photographer/Videographer at [....]. [Bridesmaid Name] to have a suitable camera/video recorder at the house to take photos/video of the bride leaving her home. The contingency for the rest of the wedding is to have an alternative standby photographer and videographer pre-selected from the guest list.

Risk No. 8. Troubles with Wedding Party Clothes or Footwear

[Bridesmaid Name] will advise the bridal party to have suitable alternative footwear accessible and she will arrange to have an emergency kit containing:

13

lipstick	gloss	blusher
stockings	hair clips	safety pins
hairbrush	hair spray	tissues
sewing kit	paracetamol	band aid
nail polish	buttons	mints

The best man will arrange to have an emergency kit containing:

comb	hair gel
paracetamol	mints

Risk No. 9. Vendors go out of business

Consider and review wedding insurance options in addition to the contingency measures and contractual arrangements entered. Use credit card to make deposits and discuss with your bank what the security arrangements are for vendors going into liquidation or closing.

Have wedding dress and bridal party attire secured and maintained as early as possible in advance of the wedding date.

Risk No. 10. No Wedding Rings

Purchased two cosmetic jewelry rings as back up. Give these to a nominated person to take to the church on the day.

1.1.4 Constraints

The project inputs explain how the product is completed and is defined, by the work breakdown structure, responsibility chart, schedule, and budget. These inputs are further decomposed into work package activities and tasks.

1.1.4.1 Work Breakdown Structure

Work Breakdown Structure WBS is a hierarchical decomposition of the wedding into work packages. It is a tree structure, which shows a subdivision of effort required to achieve the objectives. For illustration purposes we are displaying the summary level, and then the three levels below as separate diagrams.

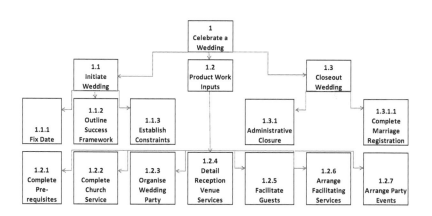

Project initiation is where all the necessary analysis is undertaken to allow the project to be planned. The WBS is a graphical illustration of the initiation process which has already been described above.

The product work inputs are the resource activities required to deliver each output objective. The product work inputs are:

Complete Pre-requisites	Complete Church Service
Organise Wedding Party	Detail Reception Venue Services
Facilitate Guests	Arrange Facilitating Services
Arrange Party Events	

The product work inputs can be further broken down into work packages and depicted graphically in a Work Breakdown Structure. The WBS below is a picture of the project subdivided into hierarchical units of work and represented as a tree.

This project close-out WBS diagram outlines the steps necessary to finalise the wedding project.

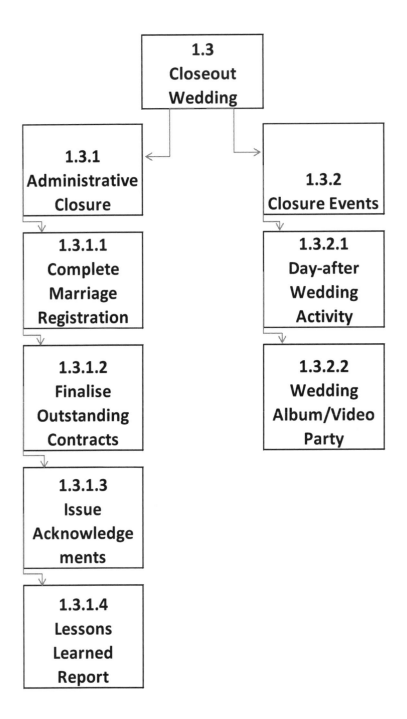

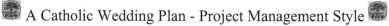

1.1.4.2 Time Schedule

A wedding ceremony is a project with a fixed end date. The Groom & Bride have determined the length of time that will be needed to complete each of the work packages given the fixed date for the wedding. The table with the start and finish dates for each activity as follows. The WBS on the left is the work breakdown structure code.

19

WBS	Description	No. Days	Time Before Wedding Day
1.1.1.1	Book Church & Priest	7	6-18 months
1.1.1.2	Book Reception Venue	20	6-18 months
1.1.1.3	Musicians Availability	20	6-18 months
1.1.1.4	Family Availability	15	6-18 months
1.1.1.5	Produce Project Charter	5	6-12 months
1.1.2.1	Project outputs	2	6-12 months
1.1.2.2	Critical Success Factors	1	6-12 months
1.1.2.3	Success Criteria	1	6-12 months
1.1.2.4	Analyse Risks	1	6-12 months
1.1.3.1	Work Breakdown Structure	10	6-12 months
1.1.3.2	Time Schedule	3	6-12 months
1.1.3.3	Resources	2	6-12 months
1.1.3.4	Cost	3	6-12 months
1.1.3.5	Procurement	3	6-12 months
1.2.1.1	Obtain Marriage Reg. Form	30	5-10 months
1.2.1.2	Do Pre-Marriage Course	50	5-10 months
1.2.1.3	Complete Pre-Nuptial Enquiry	2	5-10 months
1.2.2.1	Arrange Music & Singer	5	5-10 months
1.2.2.2	Book a Florist	3	5-10 months
1.2.2.3	Purchase Rings & Unity Candle	2	5-10 months
1.2.2.4	Pre-determine Church Seating	1	5-10 months
1.2.2.5	Organise Marriage Ceremony	10	5-10 months
1.2.2.6	Complete Marriage Reg. Form	1	5-10 months

WBS	Description	No, Days	Time Before Wedding Day
1.2.3.1	Choose the Wedding Party	10	5-10 months
1.2.3.2	Obtain Wedding Attire	40	3-6 months
1.2.3.3	Arrange Make-up and Hairstyle	3	3-6 months
1.2.3.4	Allocate Celebration Toast Roles	1	3-6 months
1.2.3.5	Produce Wedding Day Itinerary	2	3-6 months
1.2.4.1	Discuss Music Choices with Band	1	2-4 months
1.2.4.2	Choose Menu for Meal	1	2-4 months
1.2.4.3	Arrange Wine Reception	1	2-4 months
1.2.4.4	Cater for Evening Guests	1	2-4 months
1.2.4.5	Sketch Layout for Tables	2	2-4 months
1.2.4.6	Rehearse Wedding Party Entrance	2	2-4 months
1.2.4.7	Book Rooms for Wedding Night	3	2-4 months
1.2.4.8	Organise Wedding Cake	3	2-4 months
1.2.5.1	Issue Invitations to Guests	10	2-4 months
2.5.2	Invite Guests to Evening Function	10	2-4 months
1.2.5.3	Finalise Guest List	5	1-2 months
1.2.5.4	Consider Expectations	5	2-4 months
1.2.5.5	Plan Guest Table Seats	1	1 months
1.2.6.1	Book Photographer	1	3-6 months
1.2.6.2	Book Videographer	1	3-6 months
1.2.6.3	Book DJ	1	3-6 months
1.2.6.4	Book Transport for Wedding Day	1	3-6 months
1.2.6.5	Manage Wedding Day Cards	1	1 months
1.2.6.6	Arrange Payment Methods	3	1 months
1.2.7.1	Organise Honeymoon	10	3-6 months
1.2.7.2	Organise Stag Party	10	1-2 months
1.2.7.3	Organise Hen Party	10	1-2 months

WBS	Description	No. Days	Time Before Wedding Day
1.3.1.1	Complete Marriage Registration	1	1-2 months
1.3.1.2	Finalise Outstanding Contracts	2	0-2 months
1.3.1.3	Issue Acknowledgements	3	2-4 months
1.3.1.4	Lessons Learned Report	2	0-2 months
1.3.2.1	Day-after Wedding Activity	1	1 Day
1.3.2.2	Wedding Album/Video Party	1	1-2 months

1.1.4.3 Resources

The roles and responsibilities are assigned to the various members of the wedding party.

Responsibility Assignment

The Bride and Groom share most of the decision making them-selves. The Bride and Groom involve as many of their family and friends in preparing for and on their wedding day. The table outlined below can be used to depict how some of the roles and responsibilities are shared with the various family members and the wedding party. For each work package the persons with primary responsibility are the Bride and Groom. Identify additional people who may have a contribution to make to the successful completion of the work package. For example, record the initials of family or friends who have agreed to do a bible reading at the wedding and ensure that they receive a copy of the reading in advance of the wedding day.

WBS	Description	Resources
1.2.2.4	Pre-determine Church Seating	MOTB, MOTG, Groomsman 2
1.2.2.5	Organise Marriage Ceremony	Best man, Bridesmaid
1.2.3.4	Allocate Celebration Toast Roles	Best man, FOTB, FOTG
1.2.3.5	Produce Wedding Day Itinerary	Best man, Groomsmen Bridesmaids
1.2.4.6	Rehearse Wedding Party Entrance	Venue Manager, Wedding Party
1.2.6.5	Manage Wedding Day Cards	Best man, Groomsmen
1.2.6.6	Arrange Payment Methods	Best man
1.2.7.2	Organise Stag Party	Best man
1.2.7.3	Organise Hen Party	Bridesmaids

Legend: MOTB – Mother of the bride etc. Initials entered are for demonstration purposes. The key for successful completion is when everyone is aware of their respective roles.

1.1.4.4 Cost

Resource Cost

The un-denominated rates and the number of units for resources that have been determined for a fictitious wedding are:

Resource Item	Units		Total Cost
	Cost	No.	
Singer & Church Music	400	1	400
Priest Celebrant	300	1	300
Photographer	1,700	1	1,700
Videographer	1,100	1	1,100
Musicians	2,300	1	2,300
Florist	800	1	800
Transport Driver	500	1	500
Disc Jockey	400	1	400
Wedding Cake	300	1	300
Registrar	250	1	250
Pre-Marriage Course	200	1	200
Main Meal	50	140	7,000
Wine Reception	7	140	980
Evening Food	7	180	1,260
Reception Venue Rooms PP	90	12	1,080

Resource Item	Units		Total Cost
	Cost	No.	
Priest Groom Parish	100	1	100
Wedding Rings	400	2	800
Unity Candles	40	1	40
Wedding Dress	1,300	1	1,300
Bridesmaid Dresses	200	3	600
Bridal Footwear	40	4	160
Bridal Hair & Makeup	60	6	360
Bridal Costume Jewellery	10	6	60
Invitations & Postage	200	1	200
Mass Servers	20	1	20
Gifts	250	1	250
Groom Suits and Footwear	60	5	300
Flower Girl/Page Boy Attire	60	2	120
Sundry Items (ribbons for cars etc)	20	1	20
Total			**22,900**

Please note that the numbers included above are currency neutral and are for demonstration purposes only to enable costing.

1.1.4.5 Procurement

As is the case with most weddings the Bride and Groom are using contracted services and as such, they expect to

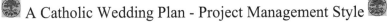

spend a lot of time and effort on procuring these services. The processes to acquire goods and services for the wedding are as follows:

1. Decide what services are required and specify the level of performance required for services.
2. Obtain quotations from 2 to 3 suppliers of each service.
3. Offer contracts following evaluation of service provider's submissions, experience, and quotations.

A sample contract is attached at appendix 1.4.3 and includes:

1. A level of detail to enable [Bride Name] & [Groom Name] match the service provided to the specifications as set out and agreed.
2. A procedure for the settlement of the contract and resolving disputes in case a dispute reaches legal proceedings and court. A resolution will depend on what is written and agreed in the contract.

1.2 Product Work Inputs

This section of the plan outlines the specifications for the product to satisfy stakeholder requirements.

1.2.1 Complete Pre-requisites

The pre-requisites for a wedding are the civil and religious requirements that must be undertaken prior to the marriage ceremony. The pre-requisites for the Bride and Groom are relatively straightforward when neither of them was married before and both are over 18 of age.

More paperwork is needed for Divorcees, Widows, Widowers, and for people who have had a former marriage annulled.

A marriage license is a document issued, authorising a couple to marry. The procedure for obtaining a license varies between jurisdictions. There are also jurisdictions where marriage licenses do not exist, and a marriage certificate is given to the couple after the marriage ceremony had taken place. The Bride and Groom familiarise themselves with the pre-requisites in the jurisdiction of their impending wedding at an early date following their intention to marry.

1.2.1.1 Obtain Marriage Registration Form

A marriage license is a document issued, authorizing a couple to marry. The procedure for obtaining a license varies between jurisdictions. There are some jurisdictions like Australia, where there is no requirement for a marriage license and a marriage certificate is given to the couple after the marriage ceremony had taken place.

In general couples must provide their marriage celebrant with a notice of intended marriage at least one month and up to 18 months before a wedding. The Bride and Groom are advised to book an appointment with the local Marriage Registrar within their jurisdiction as soon as possible to determine specific requirements. Among the items they require for this meeting are:

Birth Certificates	Revenue Insurance Numbers
Passports	Notification Fee
Wedding Date	Witnesses Details
Priest's Name	Church Location

As part of the civil registration process, the priest asks Bride and Groom to make a declaration that they are free to marry each other at the beginning of the wedding ceremony. If the Bride and Groom put together a booklet for the wedding this declaration can be included in it.

The Bride and Groom are also generally required to sign a declaration of "No Impediment" to say that neither of them is aware of any lawful impediment to their marriage. Based on all the details provided the Registrar determines if the Bride and Groom are free to marry and if so, issues them with a license or Marriage Registration Form (MRF) which is the civil authorisation for the marriage. The Bride and Groom give the MRF to the celebrant a month prior to the ceremony to check that all the details are correct before the wedding. The completed MRF is then submitted to the Marriage Registrar's Office within a given timeframe after the wedding.

1.2.1.2 Complete Pre-Marriage Course

The priest responsible for the wedding has an obligation under church law to ensure that each couple are adequately prepared for their wedding and married life. He can choose to give the marriage preparation guidance to the couple himself but generally the priest will give the couple information regarding formal courses It is therefore best to check with your priest as to the type of preparation to be undertake. Pre marriages courses can cost what the Bride and Groom can afford up to a certain maximum.

1.2.1.3 Complete Catholic Pre-Nuptial Enquiry

Like all couples getting married in the Catholic Church the Bride and Groom must complete a Pre-Nuptial Enquiry form with their local priest. Each of them must meet with a priest from their own parish who completes the Pre-Nuptial Enquiry. The Groom and Bride must provide the following documentation to their respective local priest:

a. A copy of their Baptismal Certificate
b. A copy of their Confirmation Certificate
c. A Letter of Freedom from each parish they each have lived in for more than 6 months since they were 18. The Bride and Groom may use their discretion relating to this requirement as the more parishes included means the more letters of freedom required.

This form records the fact that the Bride and Groom have been baptised, received their confirmation and are free to marry. The forms indicate that the Bride and Groom have undertaken suitable preparation and have a good understanding of the duties and responsibilities of married life. The Pre-Nuptial Enquiry forms are sent to the Parish Priest where the wedding is taking place and are retained in that parish.

1.2.2 Complete Church Service

The church service is the central part of the wedding day and provides lasting memories of the wedding ceremony. Each diocese (the region administered by a bishop) may also have its own rules regarding marriage, marriage preparation and the wedding ceremony. You will need to check with the parish priest for details about any of these additional requirements.

1.2.2.1 Arrange Music & Singer

The options usually are the local school/church choir or singer and organist/guitarist. Familiarity with performing in the church is an advantage. A do-it-yourself option is to make a CD of the music wanted and play it during the ceremony.

1.2.2.2 Book a Florist

Church flowers can be arranged by a florist or can be done by a local person who looks after the flowers in the church all year round. A popular wedding package consists of 2 pedestal arrangements on the altar area an arrangement surrounding the marriage candles, 4 pew arrangements and bows on the rest of the pews at each side of the main aisle. Some florists use flowers from those used at the church to make up bouquets for the mothers of the Bride and Groom. That arrangement can be done after the ceremony when the reception venue for the reception is close enough from the church for the florist to deliver the bouquets.

Quantities of flowers will vary depending on the size of the wedding party and personal preference. The Bride gets quotations from 3 florists for the remainder of her flowers, which may consist of bridal party bouquets and boutonnières.

The Bride arranges for these to be collected from the florists by the best man and the chief bridesmaid or other members of the wedding party the day before the wedding and delivered to their appropriate destinations or delivered by the florist. Arrange for someone with some experience to pin on the Boutonnières at the church if required.

1.2.2.3 Purchase Rings & Unity Candles

The norm for the Bride is to look for a ring to complement and fit with her engagement ring and be of a quality that neither ring would be worn down by the other if they were rubbing together. The Bride and Groom set aside a day to purchase the rings and the unity candles and maybe chill out afterwards. Rings can cost any amount, with the bride's ring normally more expensive because of the higher carat gold. The Groom gives rings to the best man before the wedding. The Bride and Groom may purchase two cosmetic jewelry rings as back up. They give these to a nominated person to take to the church on the day.

1.2.2.4 Pre-determine Church Seating

Guests at weddings have a habit of sitting towards the back of the church. The Bride and Groom may ask some of the wedding party to act as ushers to encourage immediate relatives and guests to occupy the pews directly behind them.

1.2.2.5 Organise Marriage Ceremony

Bride and Groom discuss the options for the ceremony with the priest regarding marriage vows, key prayers, and wedding songs. They decide on readers for the 1st and 2nd readings and discuss if Eucharistic Ministers can be used if there any on the guest list. The Bride and Groom may wish to produce a customised Mass booklet. The Bride's asks a couple of the wedding party to welcome the guests and present them with the mass or wedding booklet on their arrival at the church. It cannot be overstated how important it is that if someone is asked to undertake a role that they fully understand what the role entails and that they are comfortable with executing the tasks involved. A Sample booklet is attached at appendix 1.

The priest arranges a ceremony rehearsal with Bride and Groom before the wedding. He requests that the chief bridesmaid, the best man and as many others involved in the ceremony be in attendance to give them the opportunity to familiarise themselves with the church and the wedding format. This represents an excellent opportunity to iron out potential pitfalls prior to the live run.

1.2.2.6 Complete Marriage Registration Form

Bride and Groom complete the Marriage Registration Form and the best man and chief bridesmaid sign the form as witnesses. The Groom arranges for the form to be returned to the registrar during the following week.

1.2.3 Organise Wedding Party

A wedding is an affair that brings out good will in people. The Bride and Groom include as many people as possible in their wedding preparation. They attempt to share out as much as they can to their wedding party, without burdening anyone. They ensure the roles for the wedding party for the day of the wedding are well documented and straightforward. The Bride and Groom do a trial run of the wedding day, outlining the role of each person of the wedding party.

1.2.3.1 Choose the Wedding Party

The Bride and Groom ask the people they wish to have standing with them on their big day, if they would undertake the role asked of them. They decide on the size of the wedding party and whether to have a page boy/ ring bearer and/or flower girl. A rule of thumb would be to have one usher for every fifty to sixty guests, to show them to their seats and distribute mass books. Typically, groomsmen/page boys double as ushers. The number of bridesmaids/groomsmen is solely up to the Bride and Groom. The items to consider:

1. the number of your wedding party compared to the size of your guest list
2. the size of church and the altar.
3. finding and fitting dresses

1.2.3.2 Obtain Wedding Attire & Accessories

The Bride may start by looking at dresses online. It normally takes quite a few shopping trips to source the wedding dress, bridesmaid dresses, and the costume jewelry. It is best to plan shopping trips well in advance to allow plenty of time to decide. The Bride and bridesmaids may want to wear their shoes a couple of times to break them in before the wedding.

The groom can choose to purchase or hire suits for the groomsmen that may include trousers, jacket, shirt, tie, and cufflinks. The Groom can include his father and the Bride's father for the suit hire as appropriate. The groomsmen and the fathers may wear matching colour shoes of their own or hire from the suit hire shop.

The Groom organises with the shop for the suits to be in at least 1 month before the wedding to allow for fittings and any alterations. Hired suits are normally due back at the shop within 2 days. The Groom may ask groomsman to organise the pick-up and the return of the suits.

1.2.3.3 Arrange Make-up and Hairstyle

The Bride and her party agree a time and place to have their hair done and makeup applied on the morning of the wedding as appropriate.

1.2.3.4 Allocate Celebration Speakers/Toast Roles

The Bride and Groom ask the best man to act as Master of Ceremonies (MC) and control the order of events during the reception. His role is to introduce each speaker, say a few words and propose a toast to Bride and Groom. The order of speakers can vary but is agreed in advance. It is best to agree beforehand who thanks who, to avoid repetition. A popular format is:

a. Priest, Grace before meal.
b. If decided in advance during the meal the groomsmen may take turns to read out some special messages or telegrams received from overseas/relatives unable to attend etc.
c. The bride's father welcomes the guests, welcomed the groom into the family, says a few words and proposes a toast to the Bride and Groom.
d. The father of the groom says a few words and officially welcomes Bride into the family and proposes a toast to Bride and Groom.

e. The best man usually makes a short interesting light-hearted speech with humour and to the point. He proposes a toast to Bride and Groom.

f. The groom replies to the toasts on behalf of the Bride and him, and thanks both sets of parents. He compliments the Bride and thanks his groomsmen, the priest, all those who played a part in the ceremony, the staff in the reception venue and all the guests for attending. To conclude, the bridegroom proposed a toast to the bridesmaids, and thanks them for a job well done. Bride and Groom present the groomsmen and the bridesmaids with a small gift as a token of their appreciation and presented bouquets of flowers to their mothers.

g. The Bride or others may also say a few words if this is included in the plan.

h. Priest, Grace after meal.

The length of time allocated to each speaker needs to be agreed in advance as all guests may not have the same familiarity with all the speakers. You do not need guests saying it was a great wedding apart from that long boring speech by such a person.

1.2.3.5 Produce 3 Day Wedding Itinerary

The Bride and Groom with help from members of the wedding party draw up a 3-day schedule covering the day before, the wedding day and the day after. A sample for the wedding day based on the time of the ceremony at 1:30 p.m. is included below. In this scenario the Bride is leaving from her home house which is 5 minutes away from the church and the Groom is leaving from his home which is 50 minutes from the church. The Bride and Groom inform all the Wedding Party of the itinerary and give each of them a copy. The times are included for demonstration purposes.

Time	Actions for Day Before Wedding
11:30	Provide all wedding contractors with the phone number of a nominated person to call on the day of the wedding in case of an emergency.
12:00	Confirm pick-up and arrival times with wedding car company, musicians, videographer, and photographer.
12:30	Bride and Groom Pack an overnight bag for the reception and the honeymoon as appropriate.
13:30	Groom and groomsmen attend to any grooming requirements (haircuts etc.)
16:00	Sort out payment (write cheques/organise cash) for any final balances to be paid at the end of the reception
17:00	Deliver cake and any other items required to the reception venue

Time	Actions for Wedding Day
08:30	Bride and bridesmaids have hair and makeup done at the hairdresser.
10:15	Bride and bridesmaids have breakfast
10:15	Groom and groomsmen have breakfast
11:15	Groom and groomsmen get ready to leave for church.
11:30	Bride and bridesmaids get dressed
12:10	Groom and groomsmen leave for church.
12:30	Photographer arrives at bride's home
13:00	Transport arrives at bride's home
13:00.	Bridesmaid gives snacks and drinks to transport driver for the wedding party to eat while taking photographs after ceremony as required.
13:00	Priest arrives at church
13:00	Singer and organist arrive at church.
13:00	Groom and groomsmen arrive at church.
13:00	Videographer arrives at church.
13:20	Bridesmaids and flower girl arrive at the church.
13:25	Bride and father of the bride arrive at the church.

Time	Actions for Wedding Day
13:30	Wedding Ceremony begins
15:00	Wedding Ceremony ends
15:00	Guests congratulate Bride and Groom
15:45	Photographs taken at chosen location
16:45	Cocktails commence at reception location
18:00	Musicians arrive and set up
18:30	Toasts and speeches begin
18:45	Dinner is served
20:00	Cake cutting ceremony
20:45	First dance of bride and groom
21:00	Afters Guests Arrive
22:30	Tea coffee sandwiches and finger food served
23:00	DJ arrives
23:30	Musicians end for the evening
23:30	Disco Music begins
02:00	Disco Music ends

Time	Actions for Day After Wedding:
11:30	Bridesmaids take bouquets, wedding dress, and wedding cake to pre- agreed location
12:00	[Bridesmaid] takes wedding dress to be cleaned to an agreed company
12:30	Best man organised the removal of gifts from the Reception Venue
13:30	Bride and Groom check out of Bridal Suite
16:00	Bride and Groom complete business with Reception Venue manager
17:00	Bride and Groom make record of presents received in cards
21:00	Night after getting together party

1.2.4 Detail Reception Venue Services

Much of the day is spent in the reception venue and the Bride and Groom know that one of the key areas to a successful wedding from the perspective of most guests depends on their opinion of the service they receive at the reception venue. The two areas most guests comment on are the food the speeches and the entertainment. The Bride and Groom normally pay particular to detail surrounding the wine reception the meal, the speeches, evening food, the bar service, the bar extension, use of resident's bar, live music, and disco music.

1.2.4.1 Discuss Music Choices with Band

Some wedding bands can cater for all the wedding music, in the church, during the wine reception, the live music and DJ. Discussions on song and music choices are easier when dealing with one provider. The Bride and Groom keep in regular contact to discuss the music they wanted played with all the providers they are having.

Discuss the breaks and flow of entertainment with the band. Bands normally play live for two hours with a 20-minute break in between. Normally there is leeway between start and finish times. Bands performing another gig before or after yours will not have any room for maneuver as regards early/late starts or finishes. The options are many and diverse to provide alternative entertainment during breaks. For example:

1. There may be some talented dancers or story tellers in the family that could perform.
2. The Bride and Groom may wish to play CD music during the breaks.
3. Serve refreshments to guests.

1.2.4.2 Choose Menu for Meal

The manager of the reception venue with the Bride and Groom discuss and decide on the wedding menu. Reception venue managers can be extremely helpful in laying out the options for the various courses within their original quotation. The manager of the reception venue normally invites the Bride and Groom together with two guests to a meal at the reception venue to sample the wedding menu. The reception venue may agree to the Bride and Groom providing the wine. The reception venue may or may not charge corkage. The manager can advise on the number of bottles required based on the number of guests at 2 glasses of wine per guest. A sample of a wedding dinner menu is outlined in Appendix 1.4.2:

1.2.4.3 Arrange Wine Reception

The reception venue package normally includes a red carpet laid out for the Bride and Groom on their arrival at the venue. The wine reception is usually presented in a way suitable for consumption by the guests while mingling. The wine reception normally comprises of wine, punch or sparkling wine, tea, and coffee as welcome drinks for the guests on their arrival at the reception venue. The beverages can be served with sandwiches, savories, fruit, or any other combination. Some reception venues have a piano available for use during the wine reception and some venues have their own house bands that will provide musical entertainment during the wine reception. Where this is not an option it has become popular in recent times for a member or two of the band performing at the wedding to provide musical entertainment during the wine reception.

1.2.4.4 Cater for Evening Guests

The Bride and Groom may invite guests to join them for the post meal celebrations. The Bride and Groom can cater for these guests with a buffet and provide adequate table and seating space for the increase in numbers. The buffet can consist of several dishes. A popular choice is one comprising of tea, coffee, freshly made sandwiches, chicken goujons, cocktail sausages and a slice of wedding cake. Decide on a time for the buffet to be served.

1.2.4.5 Sketch Layout for Tables

The reception venue manager normally can give the Bride and Groom different dining hall table layout options based on numbers of guests. The usual criteria used to determine the most suitable layout are:

(a) guests' comfort while eating
(b) ease of movement between tables for guests
(c) catering for evening guests
(d) floor space used for dancing
(e) lighting and visibility of proceedings
(f) the wedding party entrance

1.2.4.6 Rehearse Wedding Party Entrance

Bride and Groom rehearse the format of the entrance and choose the music to be played during their entrance and the music for the entrance of the rest of the Wedding Party. "This Will Be (an Everlasting Love)" by Natalie Cole and the theme music from Rocky 11 are samples of theme music used. The preferred music can be burned on a CD. The reception venue duty manager normally agrees to set up the CD player and to do the introductions of the wedding party. The Bride and Groom can choose how creative and humorous they wish to be and what to include in introductions.

1.2.4.7 Book Rooms for Wedding Night

The reception venue manager usually advises the Bride and Groom of conditions for block booking rooms to accommodate out-of-town guests and normally allows guests booking under the Bride and Groom's name at a discount for each night stay at the time of the wedding. There may be conditions for example surrounding block booking and a timeframe within which special rate bookings can be made. Most reception venues also allow a few rooms free of charge for 2 nights as part of the package.

1.2.4.8 Organise Wedding Cake

The Bride and Groom decide on what type of wedding cake to have if any. The options for those deciding to have one are (a) the size and number of tiers (b) iced or not (c) type or types of cake, e.g., one chocolate tier, one fruit and 1 carrot (d) each tier can be made by a different person. The wedding cake is quite often made by relatives of the Bride or Groom.

1.2.5 Facilitate Guests

The success of a wedding is largely dependent on the view of the guests.

1.2.5.1 Issue Invitations to Guests

Bride and Groom make a list of guests to be invited. They record their names and addresses. They purchase or make their own invitations, put the guest names, and addresses on them and issue them. Mailing invitations remains popular despite the increasing use of email and text for replies.

1.2.5.2 Invite Guests to Evening Function

Bride and Groom made a separate list of guests to be invited to the evening function, if they choose the option for having guests attend the latter part of their wedding reception. They record their names and addresses. They purchase or make their own invitations, put the guest names, and addresses on them and issue them.

1.2.5.3 Finalise Guest List

Bride and Groom record responses to invitations. They contact guests who have not responded to their invitation, 15-20 days before the wedding date to finalise the guest count and notify the reception venue for catering purposes.

1.2.5.4 Consider Expectations

In general guests at weddings expect to feel comfortable. The following table considers the detail of other expectations.

Expectation	Action
To spend a little time with the bride and groom	Bride and Groom make a point and a plan of spending time with the guests during the day.
To have a nice meal	Have enough variety on the menu to suit most guests. If there is no vegetarian choice, then request that the chef be prepared for guests requiring vegetarian meals.
To meet up with friends and family	Bride and Groom to put a lot of thought into seating arrangements.
To relax and enjoy some entertainment	Bride and Groom choose a band to cater for the range of guests they are having.
To feel considered	Bride and Groom give directions to the church and reception venue with the invitation. Block book rooms at discount rates for guests staying at the reception venue.

1.2.5.5 Plan Guest Table Seats

The Bride and Groom can draw on their own knowledge of their guests and take on board any advice from their parents and the rest of wedding party in deciding the guest list seating arrangements. Other considerations are elbow room, couples, and families with children.

1.2.6 Arrange Facilitating Services

The range of services required for a wedding does not vary greatly. Couples can confirm the details with each of their wedding day service providers a week in advance and give them a copy of their wedding day itinerary. All the service providers are sent a pre prepared text on the day before the wedding as a reminder of the time the date and location on the wedding and a request to confirm receipt and to inform {named person} at (Mobile No) of any disruption to their planned service.

1.2.6.1 Book Photographer

A traditional photography package includes:

1. Photographs of the Bride leaving home prior to the ceremony and arriving at the Church.
2. Photographs in the church during the ceremony.
3. Photographs of wedding party at the church and at a chosen location subject to weather conditions after the ceremony.
4. Photographs of the Bride and Groom and selected guests at the reception venue. The Bride and Groom give the photographer a list of these photographs (e.g., parents, grand-parents, and godparents etc.). Assign a family member or member of the wedding party to be the

photographer's contact for gathering people together for photographs.

A basic package would include 30 of these photographs (15 pages size 30x30cms) in a bound album and a DVD of all photographs taken on the day. In the absence of a preferred photographer get 3 quotations and compare prices.

1.2.6.2 Book Videographer

With the average package the videographer would be giving the Bride and Groom 3 edited DVD copies with presentation cases of the whole day which would be approximately 3 hours, and three (3), fifty (50) minute (approx.) highlight DVD copies. The DVD would include:

Bride Getting Ready	Groom and Groomsmen at the Church
Brides Arrival	Wedding Ceremony
Signing of the Register	Bride and Groom Leaving the Church
Highlights of Photo Sessions	Wedding Party Entrance to Wedding Reception
Speeches and Toasts	1st Dance of Bride and Groom
Guest Messages	

The decision to procure the services of a videographer is based on their experience, recommendations, samples of the videographer's previous work and price. Camera work, lighting and audio quality of previous work done by the videographer for a wedding are the basic criteria for selection. The more experienced videographers will ask for details of background music they wished for the DVD in advance of the wedding and may also enquire if they could get the photographers photos to put them on the DVD.

1.2.6.3 Book Disk Jockey

The Bride and Groom may prefer a particular DJ or maybe a DJ that can perform a mixture of material to cater for all age groups that would include traditional, rock, pop, country, and soul music. In general, couples want a DJ with the experience to perform the appropriate material at the appropriate time at the right price.

When there is no one preferential DJ, the Bride and Groom start searching based on initial preferences, and recommendations from family and friends. They note email addresses and phone numbers of potential DJ's for further enquiries.

The Bride and Groom attend a few public venues to listen to the music of potential DJs. Preparing a list of questions as outlined below to ask DJ's in advance, helps narrow down the number of DJ's fitting requirements. They email or phone each DJ for answers to the questions and gather any other relevant information. The table below is a sample of criteria used in selecting a DJ for illustrative purposes:

Criteria	Unit Measure	DJ 1	DJ 2	DJ 3
No. of playing hours	No. Hrs	2	2.5	2
Sample live DVD	Yes/No	Yes	Yes	No
Travel charge	Yes/No	No	No	No
Other charges	Yes/No	No	No	No
Total price	Money	300	350	400
How much deposit	%	10	10	15
Leeway on start finish	Minutes	30	45	30
No. of breaks	Number	1	0	1
Length of break	Minutes	20	0	20
Contact for references	Yes/No	Yes	Yes	Yes
Weddings performed	Number	5	30	10
List of available dates	Yes/No	Yes	Yes	Yes
Sound limiters issues	Yes/No	Yes	Yes	No
Set up time requirement	Minutes	30	45	40

Please note that the numbers included above are currency neutral and are for demonstration purposes only to enable costing.

1.2.6.4 Book Transport for Wedding Day

Book a vintage car or other chosen method of transport to collect the Bride at her house and transport her and the person "giving her away" to the church. After the wedding ceremony the wedding party go to the locations chosen for photographs and then back to the reception venue. While there is normally no shortage of volunteers to drive the

48

bridesmaids and the groomsmen to and from the church, the designated drivers do need to be advised well in advance. Depending on the duration planned for taking photographs after the church ceremony it may be wise to nominate someone to give snacks and drinks to the transport driver for the wedding party to eat while taking photographs after ceremony. There is usually a considerable length of time between breakfast and the end of the church ceremony.

1.2.6.5 Manage Wedding Day Cards

The wedding gift of choice for many guests travelling to a wedding is a card containing money. Some couples put together a purpose made wedding card container by lining a small box with a cloth to match the colour of the bridesmaid's dresses. This card box can be left securely beside the top table or the wedding cake stand. The best man groomsman and the wedding party members are made aware of where this box is so that they can deposit cards given to them by guests or guests could drop them in the box. The best man would leave this box in a safe secure place after the meal.

If any wedding day cards are opened on the day, it is important to make a proper record of any money contained with the name(s) of the person(s) making the gift. The bride and groom may nominate a member or members of the wedding to undertake this exercise.

1.2.6.6 Arrange Payment Methods

There may be service providers that are due payment on the day of the wedding. The best man may be given charge of making payment to these providers on the day.

1.2.7 Arrange Party Events

Bride and Groom discuss party events with the wedding party. These are the informal get-togethers that help the bride and groom's family, and friends get to know each other. The best man and the chief bridesmaid generally agree to organise the stag and hen party. It has become popular to arrange an informal party for the night after the wedding for anyone wishing to come along.

1.2.7.1 Organise Honeymoon

The Bride and Groom normally book their honeymoon to start at some date after the wedding. The duration between the wedding day and the day they are going on their honeymoon will dictate what preparation by way of packing bags they do before the wedding. They make all the other necessary preparations regarding transport and accommodation and check that all their documents are in order. They obtain a marriage license and complete name-change on passport documents, if applicable.

1.2.7.2 Organise Stag Party

It is customary for the best man to organise the stag party. The best man seeks the Groom's availability, and they do up a list of their male friends they wish to invite. They discuss several options taking account of time, cost, and what they know about their friend's preferences about such things as adventure centres, rock climbing, water sports, paintballing, golf, and brewery tours etc. Based on all the information the best man collects a booking fee from everyone interested before he makes a booking.

1.2.7.3 Organise Hen Party

The chief bridesmaid arranged the hen party along the same lines as the best man organised the bachelor party. Sometimes couples end up having both parties at the same time or on the same weekend.

1.3 Closeout

Project Closeout heralds the formal end of the project. The closeout shall verify to what extent the objectives have been accomplished.

1.3.1 Administrative Closure

There are several activities that must be completed to finalise the wedding.

1.3.1.1 Complete Marriage Registration

Make a copy and submit the completed MRF to the Marriage Registrar's office as soon as possible after the wedding.

1.3.1.2 Finalise Outstanding Contracts

Pay any outstanding bills. Work on albums, DVDs, etc. with the photographer/Videographer.

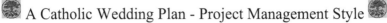

1.3.1.3 Issue Acknowledgements

Write and send thank-you cards to all who sent cards and presents.

1.3.1.4 Lessons Learned Report

Identify and record issues arising on the project. This may help to reduce or eliminate the chances of re-occurrence for friends of the Bride and Groom in the future if appropriate.

1.3.2 Closure Events

The Bride and Groom conduct any outstanding business as per their itinerary and then celebrate their achievement.

1.3.2.1 Day-after Wedding Activity

Bride and Groom implement the itinerary for the day after the wedding.

1.3.2.2 Wedding Album/Video Party

After their honey moon the Bride and Groom arrange a get together for watching the wedding video and/or looking at their wedding album.

1.4 Appendix
1.4.1 Sample Wedding Ceremony Booklet

Welcome to the

Marriage Ceremony

of

The Bride & The Groom

at

St. Mary's Church - Bridestown

on

DD/MM/YYYY

at 00.00 am/pm

Celebrant	
Best Man	
Groomsman 1	
Groomsman 2	
Chief Bridesmaid	
Bridesmaid 1	
Bridesmaid 2	
Page Boy	
Flower Girl	
1st Reading	
2nd Reading	
Prayers of the Faithful 1	
Prayers of the Faithful 2	
Prayers of the Faithful 3	
Music	

INTRODUCTION

Priest: In the name of the Father and of the Son and of the Holy Spirit

All: **Amen**

Priest: The Lord be with you.

All: **And with your spirit**

ENTRANCE ANTIPHON

Fill us with your love, O Lord, and we will sing for joy all our days. May the goodness of the Lord be upon us and give success to the work of our hands.

Lighting of the Candles

PENITENTIAL RITE

Priest: Brothers and sisters let us acknowledge our sins, and so prepare ourselves to celebrate the sacred mysteries.

All: **I confess to Almighty God and to you my brothers and sisters that I have sinned greatly in my thoughts and in my words, in what I have done and what I have failed to do: through my fault, through my fault, through my most grievous fault. Therefore, I ask blessed Mary, ever-Virgin and, all the angels and saints and you, my brothers, and sisters, to pray for me to the Lord our God**

Priest: May almighty God have mercy on us, forgive us our sins and bring us to everlasting life.

All: **Amen**

Priest: Lord have mercy

All: **Lord have mercy**

Priest: Christ have mercy

All: **Christ have mercy**

Priest: Lord have mercy

All: **Lord have mercy**

<u>GLORIA</u>

All: **Glory to God in the highest and on earth peace to people of good will. We praise you; we bless you; we adore you; we glorify you, we give you thanks for your great glory. Lord Jesus Christ, only Son of the Father, Lord God, Lamb of God, You take away the sins of the world: have mercy on us; you are seated at the right hand of the Father, receive our prayer. For you alone are the Holy One, You alone are the Lord, you alone are the most high, Jesus Christ, with the Holy Spirit, in the glory of God the Father. Amen**

OPENING PRAYER

Priest: *Let us pray:* Father, you have made the bond of marriage a Holy mystery, a symbol of Christ's love for his Church. Hear our prayers for Bride and Groom. With faith in you and in each other they pledge their love today. May their lives always bear witness to the reality of that love. We ask this through our Lord Jesus Christ, your Son, who lives and reigns with you and the Holy Spirit, one God for ever and ever.

All: **Amen**

LITURGY OF THE WORD

FIRST READING

A reading from the Book of Ecclesiasticus.

Two can accomplish more than one, for a result can be much better. If one fails, the other pulls them up. But if you fail when you are alone, you are in trouble.

Also, two gain warmth from each other. For how can you be warm alone? And one standing alone can be attacked and defeated but two can stand side by side and conquer.

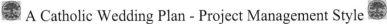

This is the word of the Lord.

All: Thanks be to God.

RESPONSORIAL PSALM

> You who dwell in the shelter of the Lord.
> Who abide in his shadow for life. Say to
> the Lord, "my refuge, my rock in whom I
> trust".

**Response: And he will raise you up on eagle's
wings. Bear you on the breath of dawn.
Make you shine like the sun and hold
you in the palm of his hand.**

> You need not fear the terror of the night,
> nor the arrow that flies by day. Though
> thousands fall about you, near you it shall
> not come.

Response: And he will raise you up on eagle's wings

> For to His angels He has given a command,
> to guard you in all of your ways. Upon
> their hands they will bear you up, lest you
> dash your foot against a stone.

Response: And he will raise you up on eagle's wings

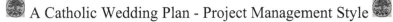

SECOND READING

A reading from the first letter of St John 4:7-12

God is love.

My dear people let us love one another since love comes from God and everyone who loves is begotten by God and knows God. Anyone who fails to love can never have known God because God is love. God's love for us was revealed when God sent into the world his only Son so that we could have life through him; this is the love I mean: not our love for God, but God's love for us when he sent his Son to be the sacrifice that takes our sins away. My dear people, since God has loved us so much, we too should love one another. No one has ever seen God; but as long as we love one another God will live in us and his love will be complete in us.

This is the word of the Lord.

All: Thanks be to God

GOSPEL ACCLAMATION   *Alleluia*

All: Alleluia, alleluia! God is love; let us love one another as God has loved us.

Alleluia!

GOSPEL READING

Priest: Cleanse my heart and my lips, almighty God, that I may worthily proclaim your holy Gospel.

The Lord be with you

All: **And with your spirit**

Priest: A reading from the Holy Gospel according to Mark.

All: **Glory to you, Lord.**

They are no longer two, but one body. Jesus said, 'From the beginning of creation God made them male and female. This is why a man must leave father and mother, and the two become one body. They are no longer two, therefore, but one body. So then, what God has united, man must not divide.'

This is the Gospel of the Lord.

All: Praise to you, Lord Jesus Christ.

Homily

THE RITE OF MARRIAGE

(The priest addresses Bride and Groom)

Priest: Bride and Groom, you have come to this church so that the Lord may seal your love in the presence of the priest and this community. Christ blesses this love. He has already consecrated you in baptism; now by a special sacrament, he strengthens you to fulfil the duties of your married life. Bride and Groom, you are about to celebrate this sacrament. Have you come here of your own free will and choice without compulsion to marry each other?

Both: We have

Priest: Will you love and honour each other in marriage all the days of your life?

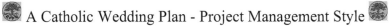

- **Both:** **We will**

Priest: Are you willing to accept, with love, the children God may give you and bring them up in accordance with the law of Christ and his Church?

- **Both:** **We are**

DECLARATION OF CONSENT

Priest: I invite you then to declare before God and his Church your consent to become husband and wife.

Groom: Bride, do you consent to be my wife?

Bride: I do

Bride: Groom, do you consent to be my husband?

Groom: I do

They join hands and say together:

We take each other as husband and wife and promise to love each other truly for better, for worse, for richer, for poorer, in sickness and in health, all the days of our life.

Priest: What God joins together man must not separate.

May the lord confirm the consent you have given and enrich you with His blessing.

BLESSING OF THE RINGS

Priest: Almighty God, bless these rings as symbols of faithfulness and unbroken love. May Bride and Groom always be true to each other, may they be one in heart and mind, may they be united in love forever, Through Christ, Our Lord.

All: **Amen.**

EXCHANGE OF RINGS

Groom: Bride, wear this ring as a sign of our faithful love. In the name of the Father, and of the Son and of the Holy Spirit.

Bride: Groom, wear this ring as a sign of our faithful love. In the name of the Father, and of the Son and of the Holy Spirit.

EXCHANGE OF GIFTS

Both: We accept these coins as a sign of sharing all that we possess.

Lighting of the Wedding Candle

SYMBOL OF UNITY

Bride and Groom extinguish the two outer candles and together, light the centre candle, symbolising their unity in marriage.

PRAYER OF THE NEWLY MARRIED COUPLE

Bride and Groom: We thank you, Lord and we praise you for bringing us to this happy day. You have given us to each other. Now, together, we give ourselves to you. We ask you, Lord, make us one in our love, and keep us one in your peace.

PRAYERS OF THE FAITHFUL

111111: For Bride and Groom, as they begin, their life together and for happiness in their home. *Let us pray to the Lord*

All: **Lord, hear our prayer**

222222: For the parents of Bride and Groom, for their friends and all who have helped them to become husband and wife. *Let us pray to the Lord*

All: **Lord, hear our prayer**

333333: For the faithful departed and especially those whom we, ourselves have loved that God will one day unite us again in the joys of our eternal home. *Let us pray to the Lord*

All: **Lord, hear our prayer**

LITURGY OF THE EUCHARIST

OFFERTORY PROCESSION
(Mothers) of the Bride and Groom (or others) take up the gifts

Priest: Pray, brothers and sisters, that our sacrifice may be acceptable to God the almighty Father.

65

All: May the Lord accept the sacrifice at your hands for the praise and glory of His name, for our good and the good of all His Church.

PRAYER OVER THE GIFTS

Priest: Lord, accept our offering for this newly married couple, Bride and Groom. By your life and providence, you have brought them together, bless them all the days of their married life. We ask this through Christ our Lord.

All: Amen.

EUCHARISTIC PRAYER

Priest: The Lord be with you.

All: And with your spirit.

Priest: Lift up your hearts.

All: We lift them up to the Lord our God.

Priest: Let us give thanks to the Lord our God.

All: It is right and just.

Priest: Father, all powerful and ever-living God, we do well always and everywhere to give You thanks. You created us in love to share your divine life. We see our high destiny in the love of husband and wife, which bears the imprint of your own divine love. Love is our origin, love is constant calling, love is our fulfilment in heaven. The love of man and woman is made holy in the Sacrament of Marriage and becomes the mirror of Your everlasting love. Through Jesus Christ the choirs of angels and all the Saints praise and worship your glory. May our voices blend with theirs as we join in their unending hymn of praise.

All: **Holy, Holy, Holy Lord, God of hosts, Heaven and earth are full of your glory.**

Hosanna in the highest. Blessed is he who comes in the name of the Lord.

Hosanna in the highest.

Priest: Lord you are holy indeed, the fountain of all holiness. Let your spirit come upon these gifts to make them holy so that they may become the body and blood of our Lord, Jesus Christ. Before He was given up to death, a death He freely accepted, He took bread and gave thanks. He broke the bread, gave it to his disciples and said:

Take this all of you and eat it: this is my body which will be given up for you

When supper was ended, he took the cup. Again He gave you thanks and praise, gave the cup to His disciples and said:

Take this all of you, and drink from it: for this is the chalice of my blood, the blood of the new and eternal covenant, which will be poured out for you and for many, for the forgiveness of sins.

Do this in memory of me.

Let us proclaim the mystery of faith.

All: **He is Lord, He is Lord. He is risen from the dead and He is Lord.**

Every knee shall bow, every tongue confess, that Jesus Christ is Lord.

Priest: In memory of His death and resurrection, we offer you, Father, this life-giving bread, this saving cup. We thank-you for counting us worthy to stand in your presence and serve you.

Lord, remember your Church throughout the world; make us grow in love, together with

Benedict, our Pope, Kieran, our Bishop and all the clergy.

Remember our brothers and sisters who have gone to rest in the hope of rising again; bring them and all the departed into the light of your presence.

Have mercy on us all, make us worthy to share eternal life with Mary, the Virgin Mother of God, with the apostles and all the saints who have done your will throughout the ages. May we praise You in union with them and give You glory through your son, Jesus Christ.

Through Him, with Him, in Him, In the unity of the Holy Spirit, All glory and honour is yours, Almighty Father, for ever and ever.

All: **Amen**

COMMUNION RITE

Priest: Let us pray with confidence to the Father in the words our Saviour gave us.

All: **Our Father who art in heaven, hallowed by thy name. Thy kingdom come, thy will be done on earth, as it is in Heaven. Give us**

this day our daily bread and forgive us our sins as we forgive those who trespass against us, and lead us not into temptation, but deliver us from evil.

Amen.

Priest: Deliver us, Lord from every evil and grant us peace in our day. In your mercy keep us free from sin and protect us from all anxiety as we wait in joyful hope for the coming of Our Saviour, Jesus Christ.

All: **For the kingdom, the power and the glory are yours, now and forever.**

NUPTIAL BLESSING

Priest: Let us ask God to bless Groom and Bride, now married in Christ and unite them in his love through the sacrament of his body and blood.

Pause for silent prayer, then the priest continues:

God, our Father, creator of the universe, you made man and woman in your own likeness and blessed their union.

We humbly pray to you for Bride and Groom, today united in the sacrament of marriage. May your blessing come upon them. May they find happiness in their love for each other, be blessed in their children and enrich the life of the church.

May they praise you in their days of happiness and turn to you in times of sorrow. May they know the joy of your help in their work and the strength of your presence in their need. May they worship you with the Church and be your witnesses in the world. May old age come to them in the company of their friends and may they reach at last the kingdom of heaven.

We ask this through Christ our Lord.

All: **Amen**

RITE OF PEACE

Priest: Lord Jesus Christ you said to your apostles: I leave you peace, my peace I give you.

Look not on our sins but on the faith of your Church and grant us the peace and unity of Your Kingdom where you live forever and ever.

All: **Amen**

Priest: The peace of the Lord be with you always.

All: And with your spirit

Priest: Let us offer one another the sign of peace.

Priest: May this mingling of the body and blood of our Lord Jesus Christ bring eternal life to us who receive it.

All: Lamb of God, you take away the sins of the world, have mercy on us.

Lamb of God, you take away the sins of the world, have mercy on us.

Lamb of God, you take away the sins of the world, grant us peace.

Priest: This is the Lamb of God, who takes away the sins of the world; happy are those who are called to his supper.

All: Lord, I am not worthy that you should enter under my roof, but only say the word and my soul shall be healed.

COMMUNION HYMNS

PRAYER AFTER COMMUNION

Priest: Let us pray. Lord, in your love you have given us this

Eucharist to unite us with one another and with you. As you have made Bride and Groom one in this sacrament of marriage and in the sharing of one bread and one cup so now make them one in love for each other. We ask this through Christ our Lord.

All: **Amen**

CONCLUDING RITE

Priest: The Lord be with you

All: **And with your spirit**

Priest: May God the eternal Father keep you steadfast in your love

All: **Amen**

Priest: May you have children to bless you, friends to console you and may you live in peace with all people

All: **Amen**

Priest: May the peace of Christ dwell in your home. May the angels of God protect it and may the Holy family of Nazareth be its model and inspiration.

All: **Amen**

Priest: May almighty God bless you, the Father, the Son, and the Holy Spirit

All: **Amen**

Priest: The mass is ended. Go in peace to love and serve the Lord

All: **Thanks be to God**

Signing of the Register

Recessional

1.4.2 Sample Wedding Day Menu

<u>*Bride & Grooms Wedding Dinner Menu*</u>

<u>*Starter*</u>
Chicken & Mushroom Vol au vent
Or
Garlic Mushrooms

<u>*Soup/Sorbet*</u>
Cream of Vegetable Soup with Parsley or
Raspberry Sorbet

<u>*Main Course*</u>
Poached supreme of Irish Salmon with a light lemon-dill sauce
Or
Prime Roast Sirloin of Beef with Roast Shallot, & Horseradish Sauce
Or
Traditional Roast Turkey & Ham with Sage & Onion Stuffing
All Served with a
Selection of Market Fresh Vegetables and Potatoes

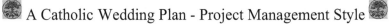
<u>*Dessert*</u>
Baked Apple Crumble with Vanilla Anglaise
Or
Profiteroles with fresh Cream and Chocolate Sauce
Or
Medley of Desserts (3 mini desserts)

<u>*Freshly Brewed Tea / Coffee*</u>

1.4.3 A Sample Contract

[Service Name] Contract

This agreement is between [Bride Name & Address] & [Groom Name & Address] and [Service Provider Company Name & Address], represented by [Service Provider Manager Name & Address]. By signing this document, the parties agree that the terms outlined herein are acceptable.

[Bride Name] & [Groom Name] engage [Service Provider Company Name] to provide [general description of service] with the following specifications:

[Detailed description of service, to include price, timelines, payment terms, deposit, location, cancellation process, dispute resolution]

Signed

Bride Signature	
Bride Contact Number	
Groom Signature	
Groom Contact Number	
Service Provider Signature	
Service Provider Name	
Service Provider Contact No.	
Date	

Printed in Great Britain
by Amazon